This book belongs to...

The Seashore Fairies™

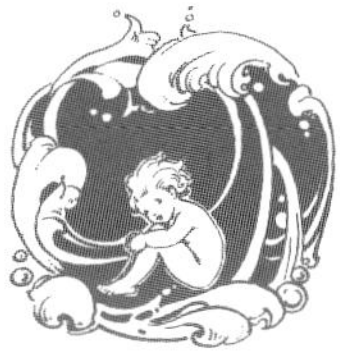

Illustrated by

Margaret W. Tarrant

Original poetry by

Marion St. John Webb

Series Editor

Fiona Waters

MP

MARGARET TARRANT'S™

FAIRIES & FLOWERS

First published in this format in 2002 by
The Medici Society Ltd
Grafton House, Hyde Estate Road, London NW9 6JZ

First published in 1925 by The Medici Society Ltd
1 3 5 7 9 10 8 6 4 2

A catalogue record for this book is available from the British Library.

ISBN 0 85503 253 7

Margaret Tarrant's original artworks have been rescanned for this re-designed edition.

Designed by Tony Potter Publishing Ltd

Printed in Singapore

The
Seashore Fairies™

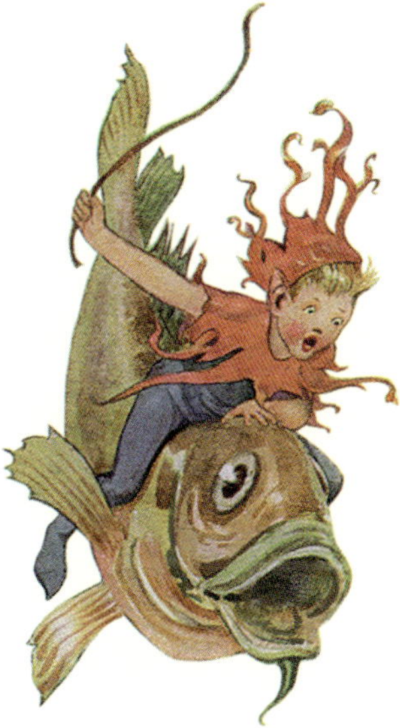

Margaret Winifred Tarrant (1888 - 1959)

'Every time a child says, " I don't believe in fairies," ' warned Peter Pan, 'there is a little fairy somewhere that falls down dead.' By her paintings Margaret Tarrant did as much to stop this happening as J M Barrie did by his writings. Born in London in 1888, the only child of artist Percy Tarrant and his wife Sarah, Margaret excelled at art from an early age, and she was only 19 when she received her first, very prestigious, commission, from J M Dent & Sons: to illustrate Charles Kingsley's much-loved children's classic, *The Water Babies,* which was first published in 1863.

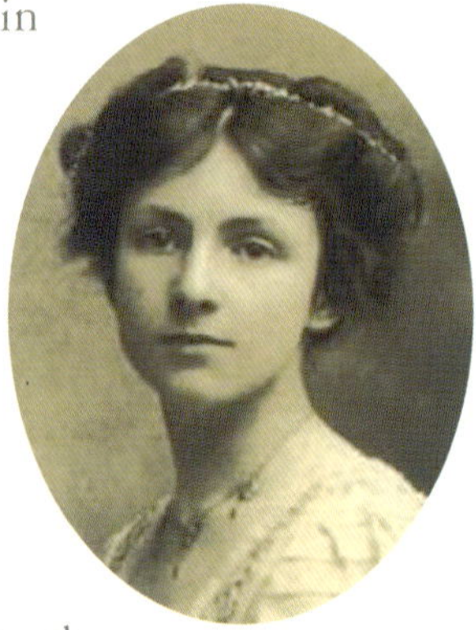

Her delicate, charming pictures matched the spirit of the story perfectly and earned her a string of new commissions: *Nursery Rhymes* (1914 and 1923), *Alice in Wonderland* (1916) and *Hans Andersen's Fairy Tales* (1917) for Ward Lock & Co., plus postcards for Oxford University Press.

She illustrated some 20 books for George G. Harrap & Co. between 1915 and 1929, but an even more important publishing relationship began in 1920, when she did her first pieces for The Medici Society. This was to prove a long and fruitful connection, resulting in most of her best-known work. In the 1920s, for example, she illustrated this highly successful series of fairy books for the company, written by the poet and author Marion St John Webb. Her picture of Peter's Friends, inspired by J M Barrie's *Peter Pan* stories and the statue in Kensington Gardens, proved so popular when it appeared in 1921 that it had to be reproduced many times.

In the following year, her *Do You Believe in Fairies?* showed two children encircled by a ring of fairies and caught the public excitement created by Sir Arthur Conan Doyle's 1922 book *The Coming of the Fairies,* a true account of two young girls in a Yorkshire village who regularly saw fairies.

During her life Margaret Tarrant tackled a wide range of subjects and won special acclaim for those, such as *All Things Wise and Wonderful,* with a religious theme. But her forte was fairies, for in her evocation of these ethereal figures she could express her love for children, wild flowers and dance, of all that was beautiful and pure. She would sketch meticulously from life to capture the likeness of a child or plant, then compose her pictures by arranging the subjects in imaginary settings, infusing them with a distinctive otherworldly quality. Her fairies have a unique fluidity and balletic grace that expressed her delight in the free-flowing dance invented by Isadora Duncan.

Margaret Tarrant was very much a free spirit herself, flying along the country lanes around her home in Surrey on an ancient bicycle, leaping off impulsively to sketch a flower or help a toddler to paint. She never married, but she attracted many friends by her generosity, energy and zest for life. Perhaps it was this childlike enthusiasm and innocence, combined with a special kind of imagination, that gave her a natural affinity with fairies.

Much missed when she died in 1959, she left a lasting legacy in charming pictures that seem as fresh today as the day they were painted, and still enchant new generations with their glimpses into a secret fairy world.

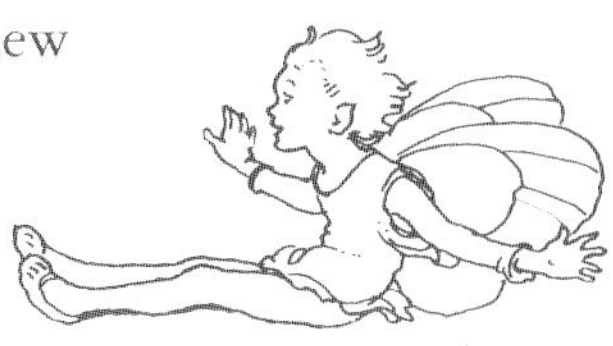

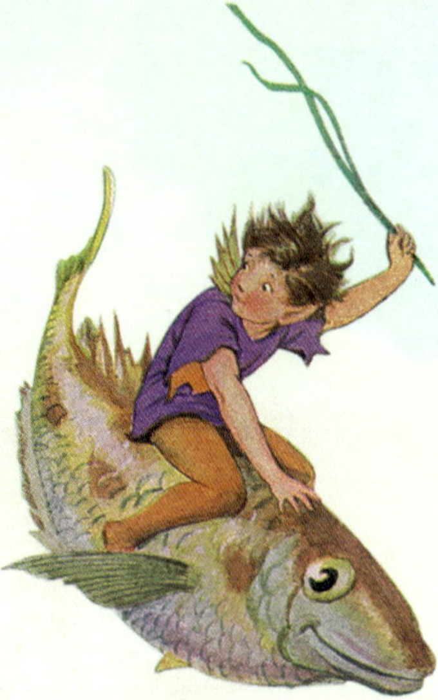

Contents

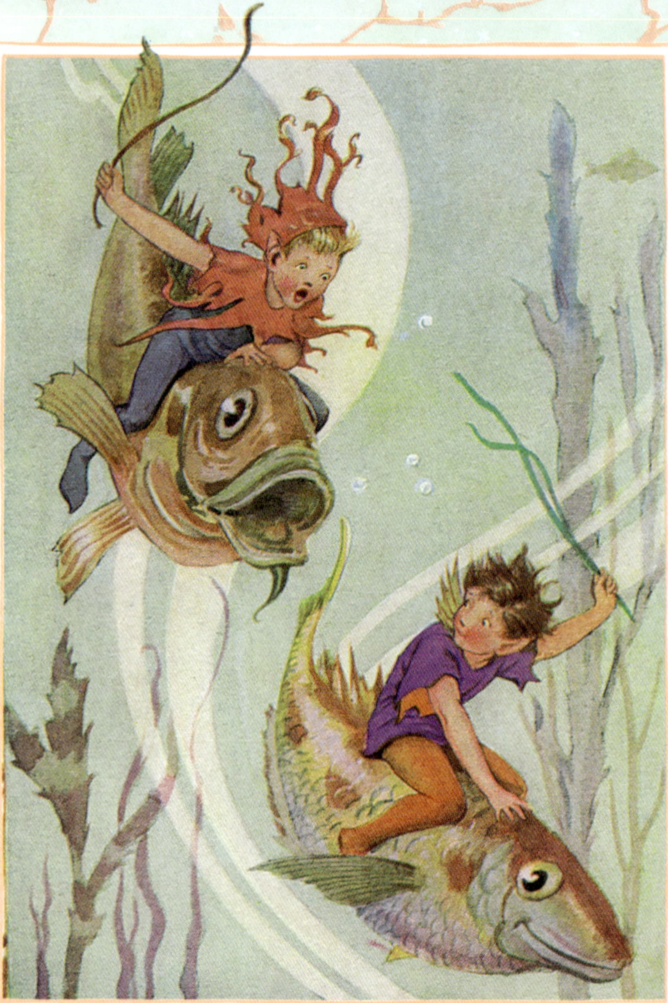

The Shell on the Mantelpiece

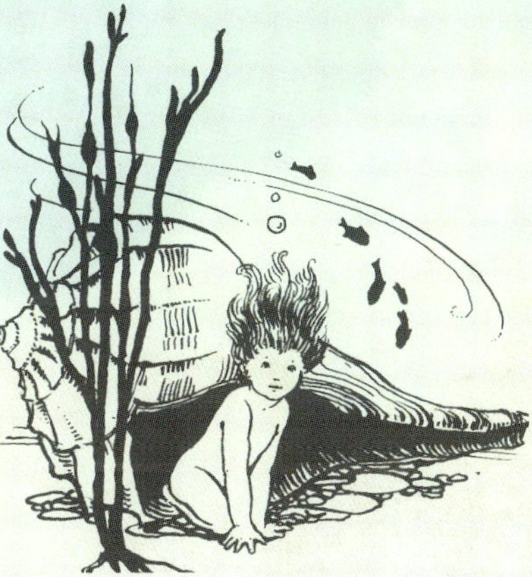

There is a little cottage
On a cliff beside the sea.
And the cottage has a kitchen
Where sometimes we have our tea;
And the kitchen has a mantelpiece
With such a clutter all along,
Photographs, letters and seaweed
And a clock that's always wrong.

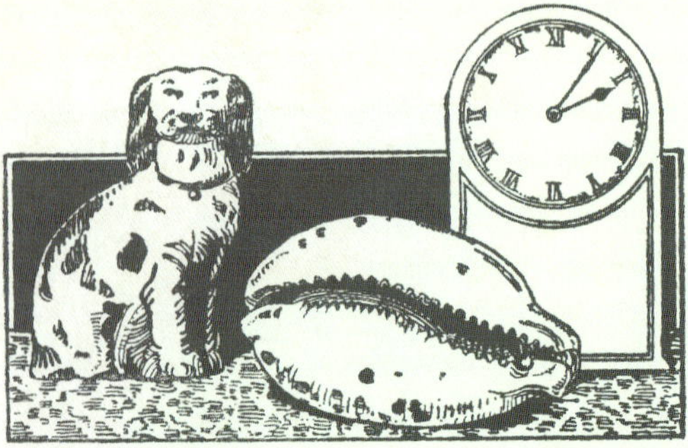

And there, shining in the corner,
Just beside a pretty cup,
Is a lovely, pearly seashell,
Which oh! so carefully I pick up.
I take it to the window
To look far out across the sea.
And then I hold it to my ear;
It whispers such tales to me!

And I have heard the story
Of the cod whose eyes were odd,
And one eye was a magic eye,
The other - simply cod.
And with his magic eye he'd see
The Sea Fairies passing by;
But only fish and seaweed
Could he see with the other eye.

And I've been told the stories
Of the Seaweed Fairies' races,
Upon the backs of flying fish
With friendly smiling faces.

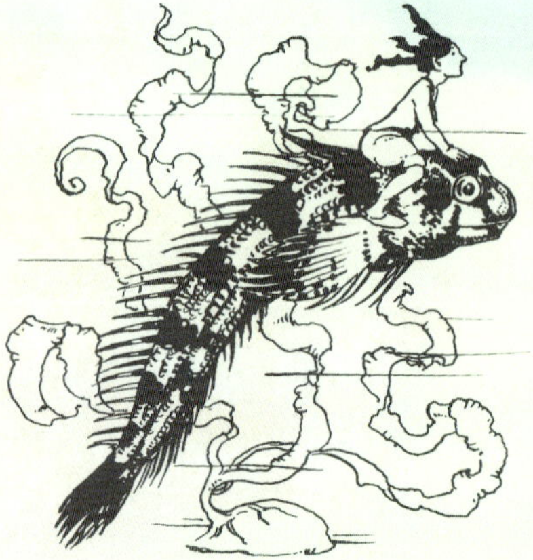

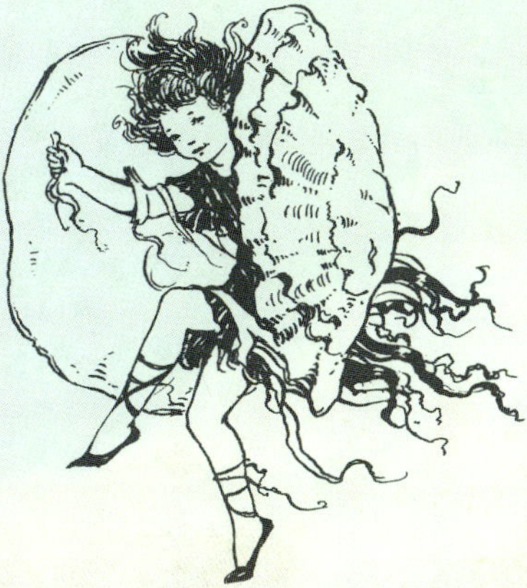

And of when the Oyster Fairies
Went dancing through the waves.
All the limpets turned their heads,
And laughed from inside their caves.

I've heard about the starfish
Who wanted to catch a star
He saw one reflected in the sea
And tried to keep it in a jar . . .
And tales about sea-urchins
Who were naughty as could be!
And lobster tales, and winkle tales -
All these the seashell told to me.

So many tales - so many tales . . .
Some very short - some very long -
Inside the little kitchen
Where the clock is always wrong.

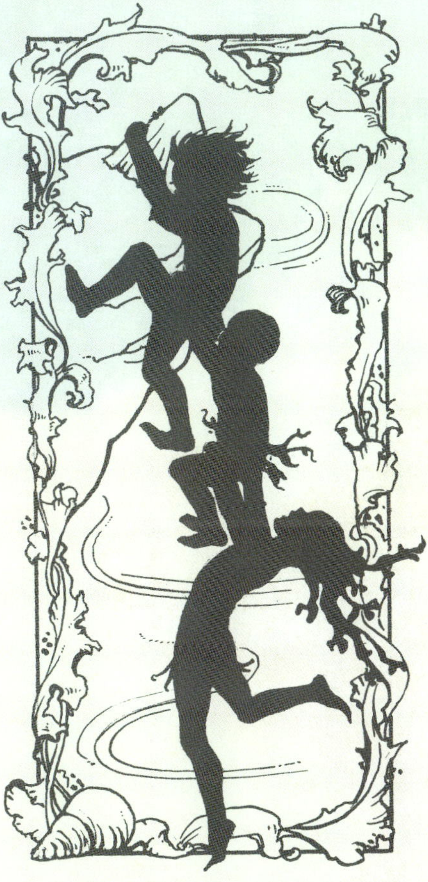

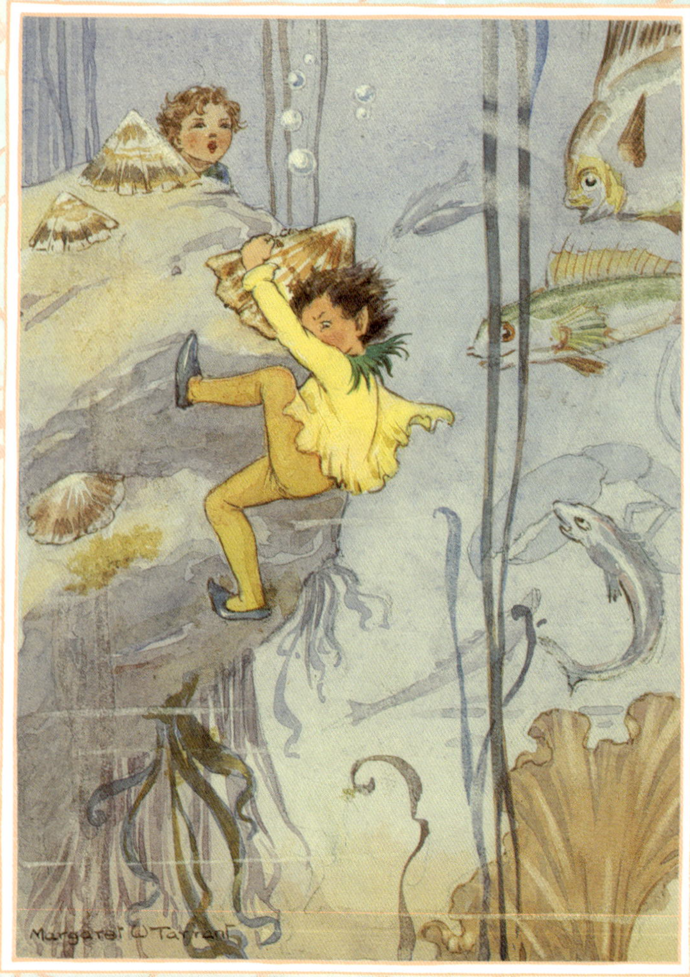
Margaret W Tarrant

Miss Letty

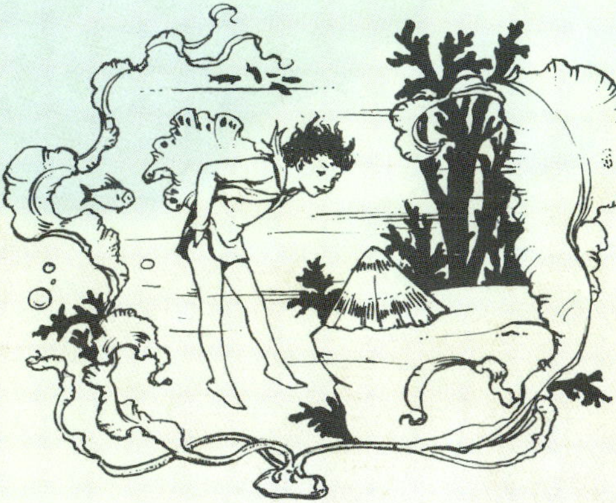

Miss Letty was a limpet
Who chose to make her home
Upon a piece of jagged rock,
Beneath the ocean foam.
And she was kind and friendly,
So asked her friends to tea.
She gave them tuna sandwiches
And teapots full of sea.

Miss Letty was a limpet
Her shell was like a hat.
It fitted snug and very tight
When on the rock she sat.
As he went swimming by,
A Seaweed Fairy said,
"Now that's a lovely hat!
I shall wear it on my head."

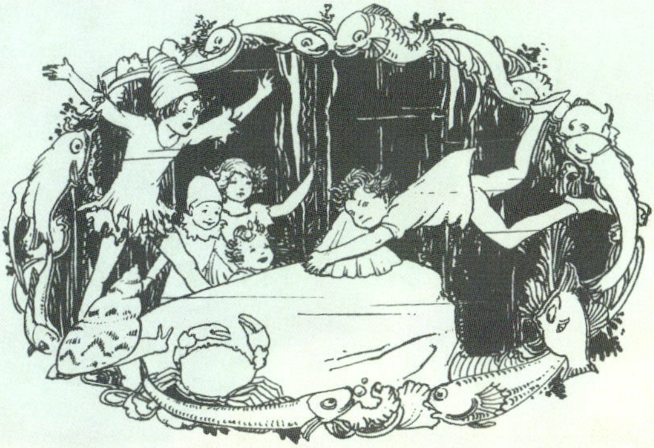

So thus began the tussle
That lasted for a year.
And fairy folk and fishes came
From far and wide to cheer.
The Seaweed Fairy pulled and pulled
Miss Letty held on tight!
The Seaweed Fairy tugged and
tugged
He strained with all his might.

One day a handsome lobster
Came up, and said he'd found
The rock Miss Letty lived upon
Was his. "It's private ground!"
He built a wall of winkles
To keep the fairies out.
Unless they paid to come inside
They'd have to do without.

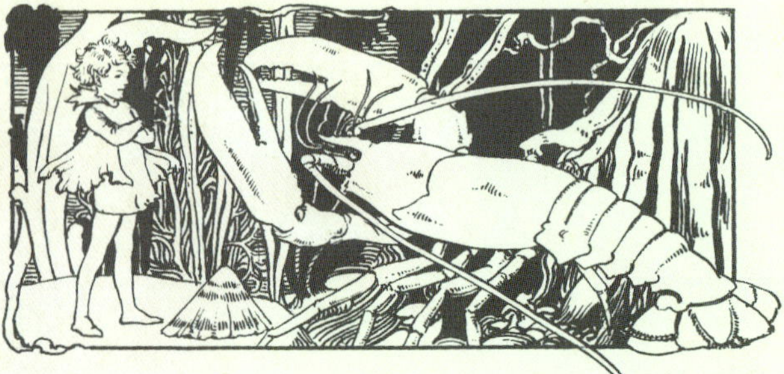

He said the smallest fishes
Could come for half the price.
So everyone was satisfied
And thought him very nice.
He sold a season ticket
Which was valid for a year
So fish and fairies all alike
Could sit and watch and cheer!

At last the Seaweed Fairy
Gave up his hold and cried,
"Miss Letty's won the battle!"
The news spread far and wide.
Then fishes, fairies, and the
  winkles,
All crowded round to see.
But all Miss Letty longed for
Was a teapot full of sea.

Miss Letty was a limpet,
Who chose to make her home
Upon a piece of jagged rock,
Beneath the ocean foam.
And there she stayed for ever
As she knew all along
No fairy lived that could her budge
For limpets are too strong!

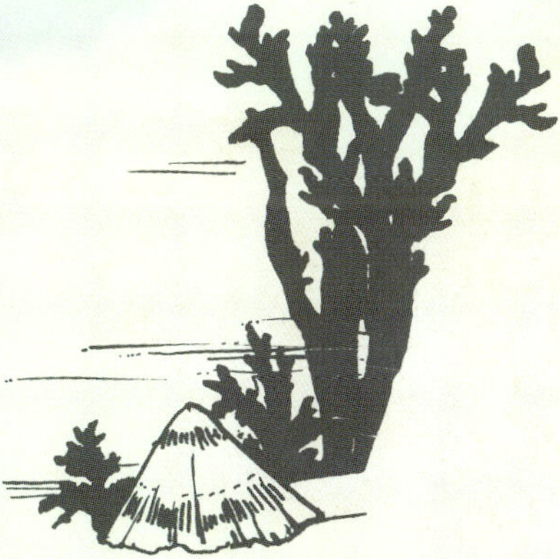

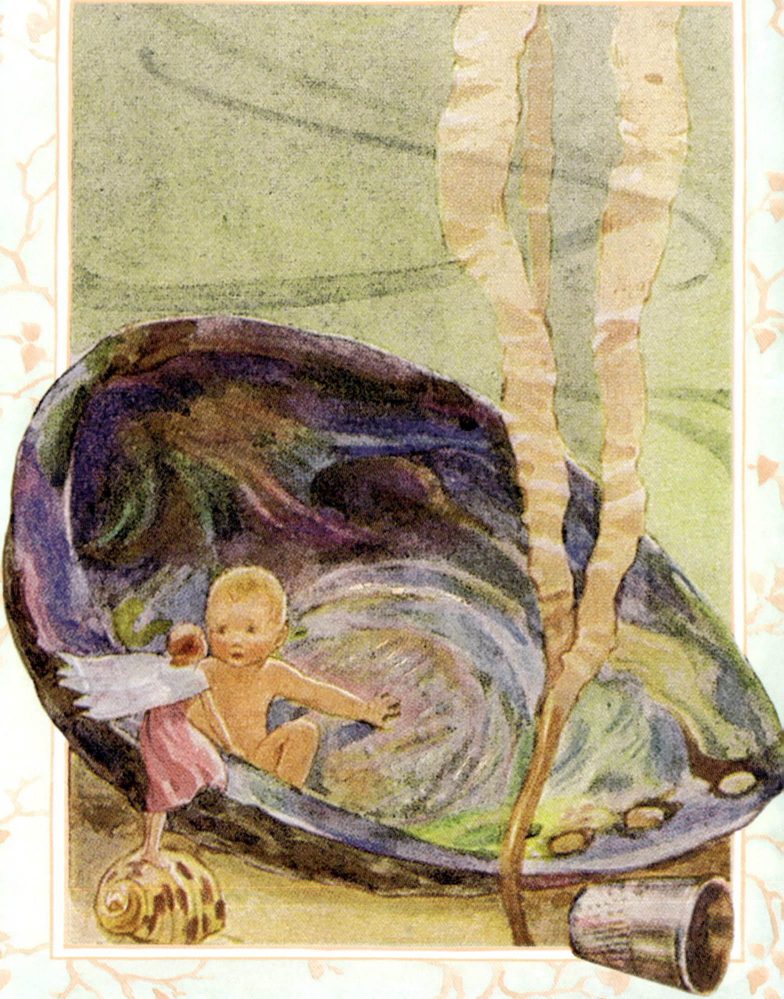

The Littlest Fairy

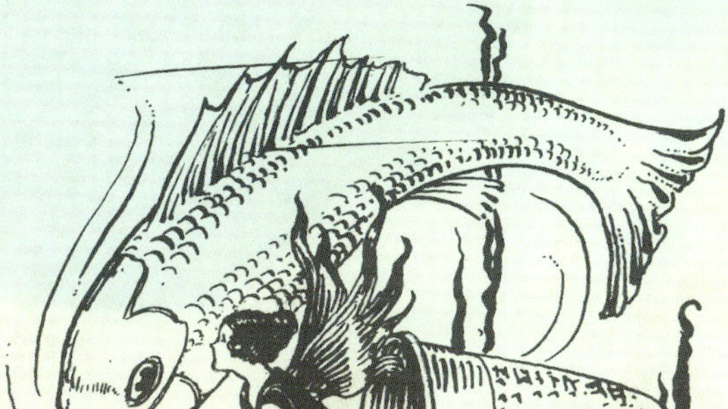

The Littlest Fairy in the world
Lives underneath the sea.
And nobody knows how old she is,
Nor why she is so wee.
She lives inside a thimble that
A lady dropped, they say,
From out of a great big ship that
went
Sailing past one day.

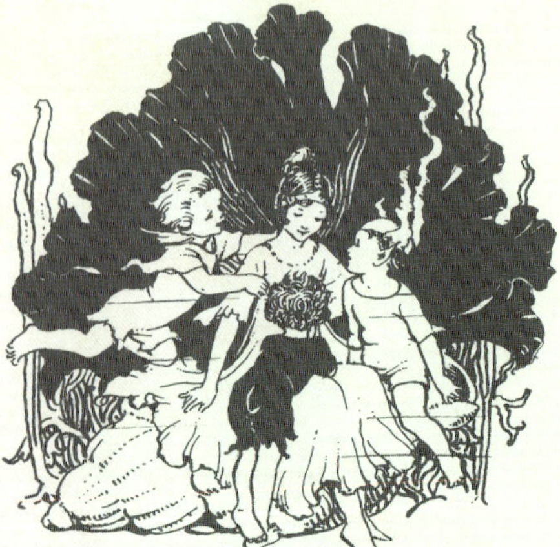

The Littlest Fairy in the world
Is kind to all small things;
She is specially good with tiny fish,
And fairies with no wings.
And if ever a baby starts to cry
She quickly whispers in its ear
"Hush, the Littlest Fairy's here!
Now you have nothing at all to fear."
And everyone's troubles are easier to
bear,
They say, when the Littlest Fairy's
there.

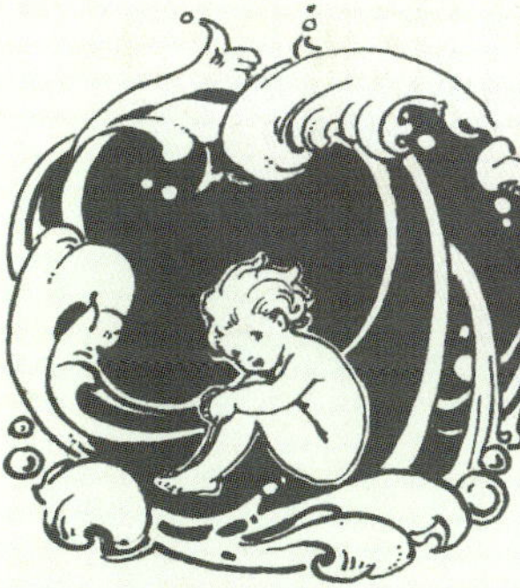

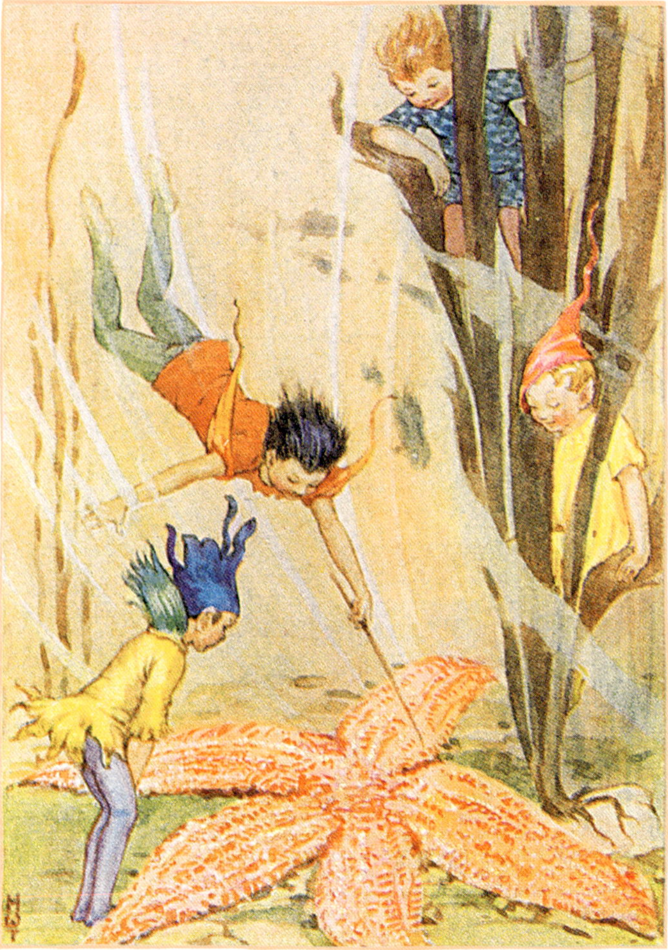

Once there was a Starfish

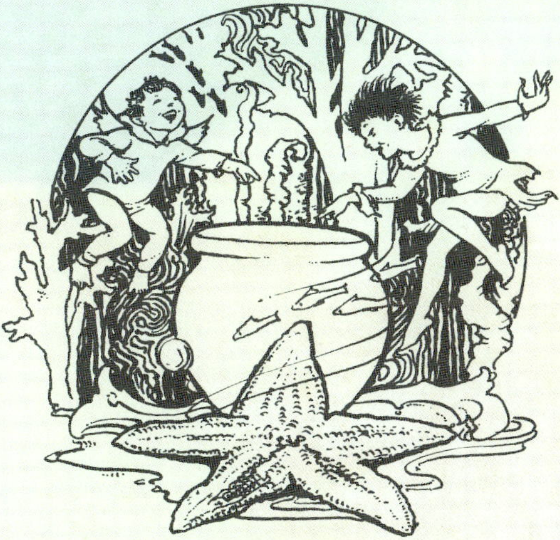

Now once there was a starfish
Who tried to catch a star.
It was reflected in the sea
So he popped it in a jar.

He caught the star's reflection
And in the jar it shone,
But when next morning came
He found the star had gone.

Next night he caught the star again
And in the jar it shone,
But then once more he fell asleep
And by the morning it was gone!

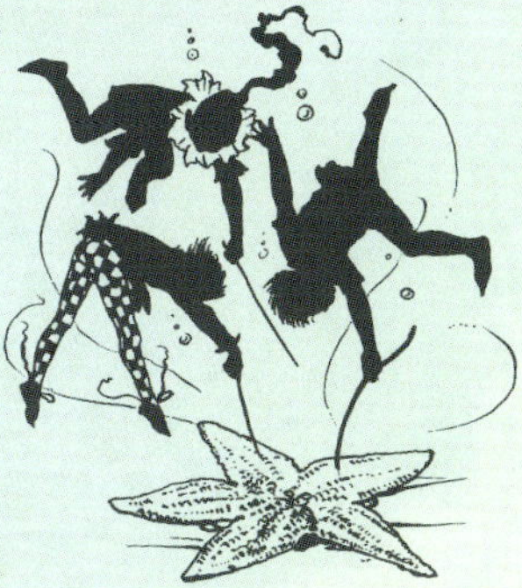

And so he asked the fairies
To come and shout and shake,
To tickle him the whole night long,
And keep him wide awake.

The fairies, much delighted,
Worked hard and well and long.
And every time they tickled him,
They sang a noisy song:

"Wake up! Wake up!
You sleepy head!
You've lost the star
You caught in the jar!
Wake up! Wake up!
You sleepy head!"

The starfish lost his sleep,
He also lost his star,
For when next morning came around
He found an empty jar!

But now his great-grandchildren
Will show the jar with pride,
And tell how their great-grandpapa
Once caught a star inside.

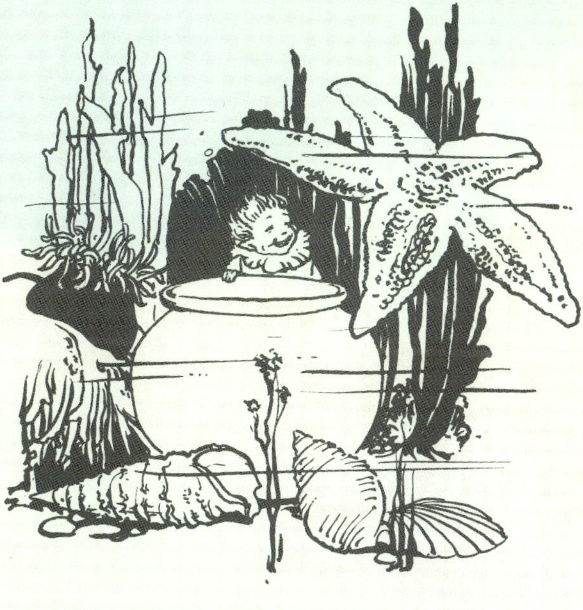

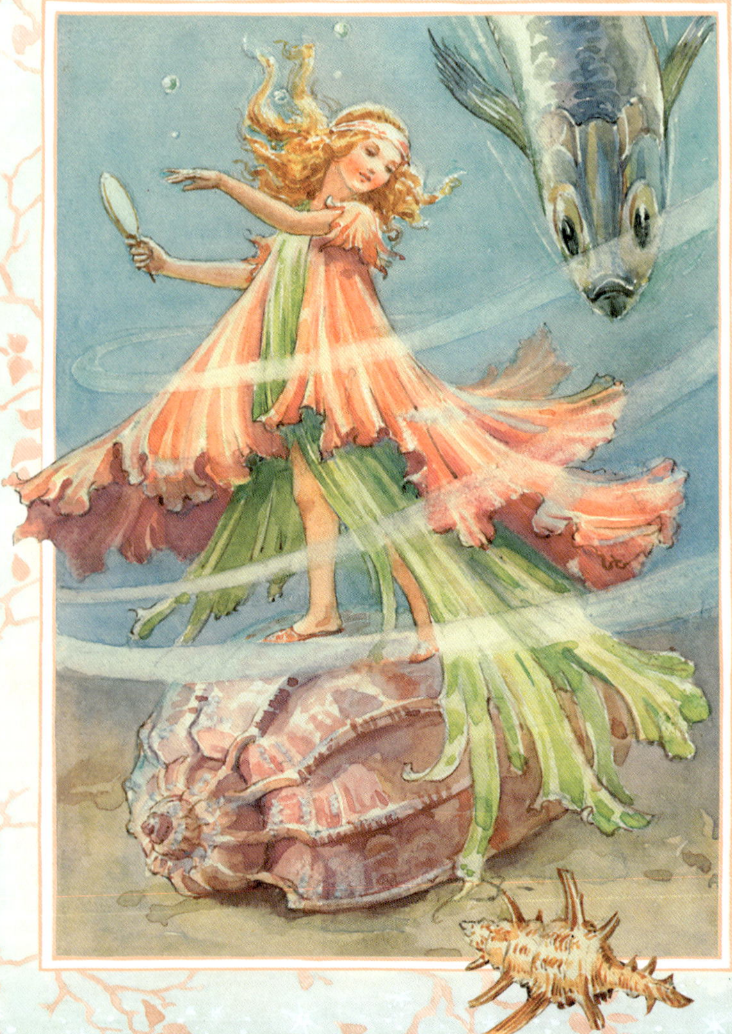

The Seaweed Dress

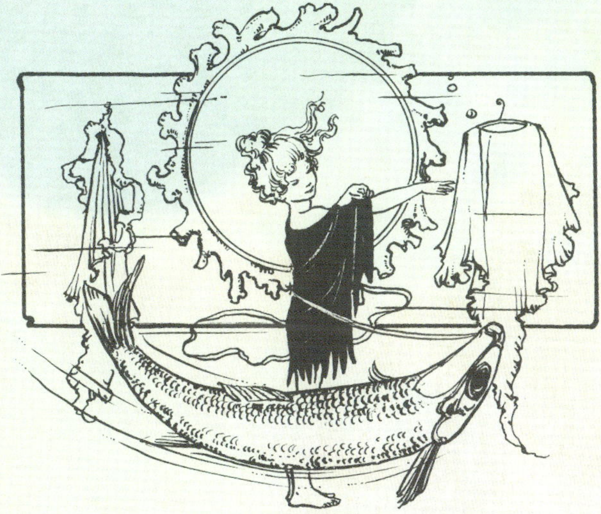

Inside her little coral house
Miss Herring worked all day and night.
Her stitches were small and neat,
Her silky dresses soft and bright.
The clothes she made! Ah, how I wish
That I had been a little fish!

She made a dress of lacey foam
And one of pearls and oyster shells.
A golden one of shimmering sand
And one all covered in tiny bells.
But loveliest of all the frocks
Was specially for the Fairy Silverlocks.

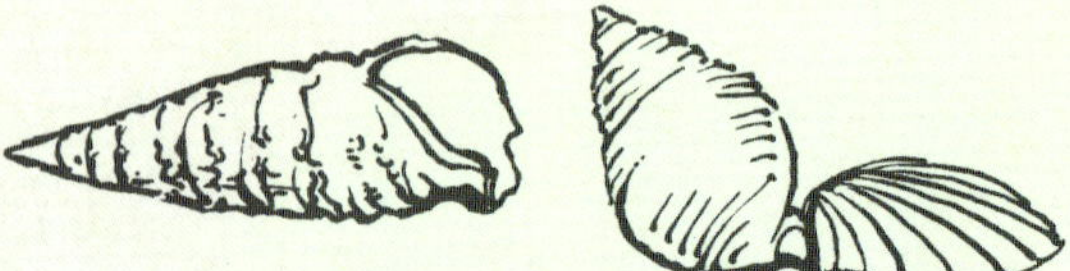

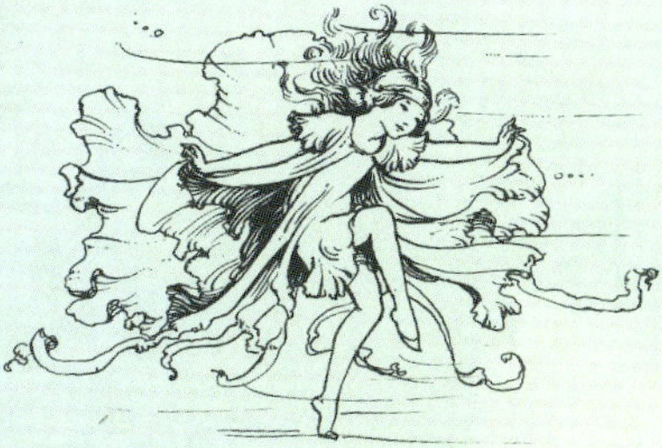

The Fairy Silverlocks was asked
If she would dance and sing
At Lady Haddock's special tea
For the birthday of the Cockle King.
The fairy nodded her silver head.
"I will do so with pleasure," she said.

Then she hurried to Miss Herring's house.
"I need one of your special frocks!"
"A seaweed dress, I think," Miss Herring said.
"You will look lovely, I promise, Silverlocks."
Miss Herring stitched and stitched some more
Then worked harder than ever before.

The seaweed dress was wonderful,
And beautiful to see.
And nothing else was talked about
At Lady Haddock's tea
Except the dress of fine seaweed green,
A dress that might be worn by a queen.

The Cockle King rose to his feet
And smiling gave his hand
To Silverlocks, as she danced there,
Twirling over the sand.
And very brave he must have been,
For Silverlocks became his Queen.

Miss Herring pinned a notice up:
"By Royal Appointment to
Her Majesty the Cockle Queen."
And so her fame it grew,
Until all the fishes came in flocks
To buy Miss Herring's seaweed frocks.

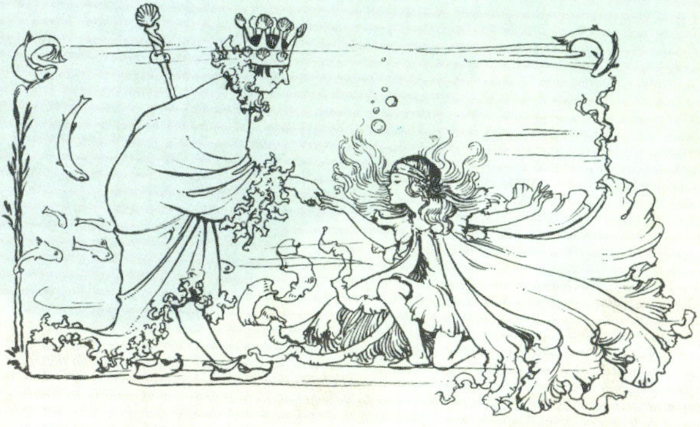

Inside her little coral house
Miss Herring works all day and night.
Her stitches are small and neat,
Her silky dresses soft and bright.
The clothes she makes! Ah, how I wish
That I had been a little fish!

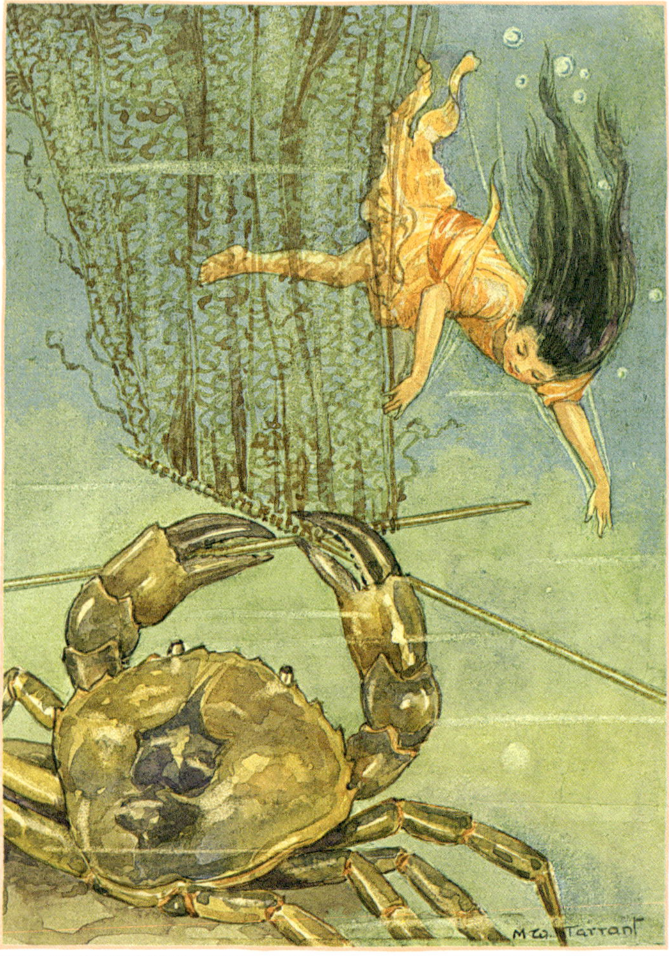
M.W. Tarrant

Dropping Stitches

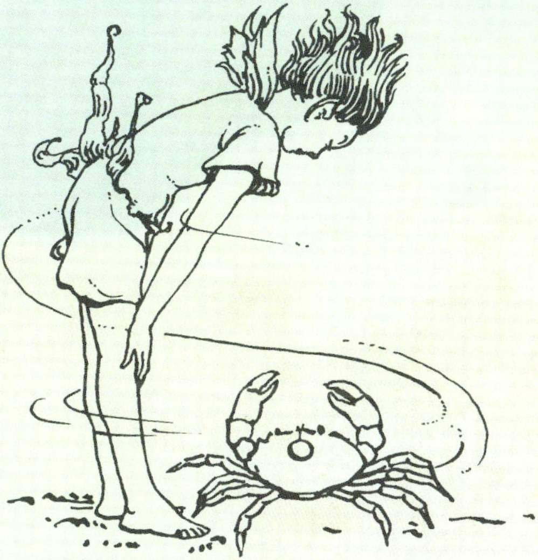

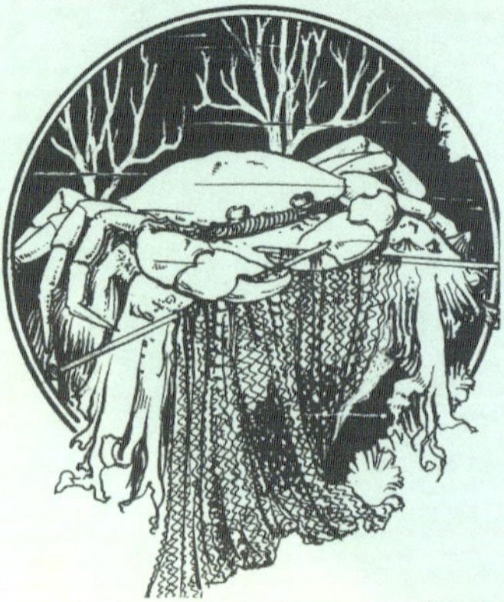

There was a crab called Bertie,
Who longed for fortune
and fame.
"If I knit a coat of seaweed
All the sea will know my name!
I'll send the coat, when finished,
To the King of all the Fishes,
With compliments respectful,
And cheerful birthday wishes."

He'd gathered lots of seaweed
And wound it in a ball
But then he dropped some stitches.
This wasn't planned at all!
He tried to catch them quickly,
But in spite of all his cunning
The seaweed was too slippery
And the stitches went on
running, running.

Bertie grew all hot and bothered
And then began to cry.
"It isn't fair," he whimpered,
As he rubbed and rubbed his eye.
He cried, and went on crying
For a fortnight without stopping.
And everyone came looking,
While the stitches went on
dropping, dropping, dropping.

And as he went on weeping,
Whispers grew across the land.
"He'll make the sea so big that
It will swallow all the sand!
And all the dry-land creatures
Into the sea will come flowing.
There won't be any room left!"
And the sea kept growing,
GROWING . . .

The fishes gathered round him,
And they begged him not to cry.
The starfish lost their glow
And the limpets gave a sigh.
The fairies coaxed and argued,
But Bertie went on crying.
People came to stop and stare,
Still Bertie went on weeping!

The lobsters tried to stop him,
But Bertie cried some more.
The minnows came in shoals
And sat outside his door.
With all these people gathering,
The noise became quite loud.
Bertie said, "I must be getting
famous.
Perhaps I should be proud."

The sponges came in dozens,
But they mopped and mopped in vain.
They couldn't dry his tears up,
So they squelched away again.
Then the fairies made a medal,
And the King of all the Fishes
He presented it himself.
"For you, Bertie, with good wishes!"

Then Bertie did stop crying.
"At last, fame has come to me!
And simply by dropping stitches
I am known throughout the sea."